After Phinehas

Eli Stok

BookLeaf Publishing
India | USA | UK

Presentation by *BookLeaf Publishing*

Web: www.bookleafpub.com

E-mail: info@bookleafpub.com

ISBN: 978-93-5744-935-9

First edition 2022

to Ron Cole,

gentlest of teachers

ACKNOWLEDGEMENT

I would like to thank all the people who saw "behind the mask", who listened to me and gave me space to put my thoughts into words, no matter how inchoate, raw, or unorthodox.

You know who you are. Thank you.

PREFACE

The poems in this volume were mostly born
from struggle; the struggle of being a persona as
well as a person, of representing an institution
that both fascinates and repels, that is cherished
by some as essential for life and is safely
ignored by many others.
It may be that the alienation, the defiance, the
agonizing struggle with the sources, but also the
occasional note of tender and fragile longing,
will strike a chord with some readers.

Tailoring wisdom

Voluminous billowing cloth that can embrace
all forms; sparkling in light of early morn;
true image of the folds of time and space –
the cloak of erudition lightly worn,
clasped and adorned with geometric gems
completed by a ruby at the heart,
vital eccentric centre. At the hems
seven dancing bells that resonate. In part
this intricate stitchment of energized human
    signs
seems like a yarn spun on the looms of God.
The chasubles, worn by our own divines,
present this cherubic aspect. Feet wing-shod
flutter beneath in ill-disguised employ:
a blessing on the gospellers of joy!

Mask

When rising from the stone cathedral floor,
receiving cup and plate in oily hands,
one is supposed to host a something-more,
a gift, a power on which loads of demands
may lawfully be placed. Or, matter-of-factly,
one is regarded as a central node
(however tidy one's religious act be)
of churchly protocols. And in this mode
the surface of my skin somewhat extends,
reflecting what's expected, flowing smooth
like folds of chasubles, without loose ends
that, tugged, might ravel into doubtful truth.
Friends, I go much more gladly to my task
because you see my face behind the mask.

St Hubert's Day

sweet this young face
to transmit folklore
forgotten and dug up

blessing the freshly baked bread
in a bakery

smiling pride in an ancient profession
displayed to an alien visitor
surprised by his own dignity

what could go wrong

but the folklore is ritual
and ritual is dialogue
and the responses are lost

and the sacredness of the young father's hand
over the daily bread of life
is scattered by the great-grandfatherly words
of the prescribed blessing in the book

presupposing loyalty
to a shared god
unbreakable like old bread

attention flags
and the second blessing
no longer expected or desired
of the people who make the bread
with a powerless sign of the cross
feels like invading
good people on their home turf

it could have been worse
the pictures were nice
they were on Instagram

Funeral Scriptures

now as to further dignify this funeral
might i suggest a reading from the sacred
    scriptures
that have brought comfort to many grieving
    souls
and odor of salvation to a weeping world

which one would you prefer

there is the one from the happiness speech
blessed are the poor in spirit
blessed are those who mourn

no i understand your reluctance
death is no time for paradox

well how about the supper speech
the father's house has many mansions
no one comes to the father but through me

on the various shades of religious sensibility
among those present i wish to cast no aspersion

there is the story of a death
where after a man's final tortures

a nearby curtain splits asunder

the circumstances of his passing
i agree are not at all analogous to your father's
    demise

well what about the hopeful sequel
two travellers in grief and doubt
joined by their friend who is risen from the dead

your son is traumatized by zombies
i see

then the wheat grain that falls in the earth
and dies to bear fruit
because whoever hates his life will keep it

this does seem ill-fitting
for one who loved life so much

the servants who keep watch
and see their master gird himself and serve
arriving at the unexpected hour

although considering the circumstances
unexpected might not be the adequate word

how about: the last enemy to be destroyed is
    death

because he has subjected everything to his
    power
(except of course the one who subjected
    everything to him)

it is a rather convoluted discursion
on such an emotional day

something simpler and more charitable then
no one lives or dies for himself alone, but for the
    lord
and we shall all appear before his judgment seat

yes i understand your loving memory
does have something final about it

this for finality: we have passed from death to
    life
we know because we love our brothers (and
    sisters of course)
everyone who hates his (or her) brother (or
    sister) is a murderer

indeed the sacred space of grief
is ill adorned with discussion of crime

how about: i lay down and slept
i woke again, for the lord sustained me
you strike all my enemies on the cheek

of course your father's temper
has not granted him many enemies

another poem: as a deer pants for flowing
    streams
so pants my soul for you, o god
when shall i come and appear before god

no indeed there is no question of when
if there is heaven then there is he

and for the funeral
we shall read the poem by rupi kaur
"the universe took its time on you"

Thoughts in a long moment

And no doubt there was a time
when poets invoked a goddess
of words – but please. There is so
much input already. And I am only
here because I feel strange. An old
man does not catch butterflies. When are you
old? Is it
when you understand Saturn swallowing
his vivid outcasts because they were after all not
    exactly
true to type?

Because you see, there is light, there has
to be. But it is difficult to tell the stars apart
from the constellations – after all, what is there
to tell. And who would survive the shock
if the Great Bear were torn apart? Even
with nuance and precision. Well, I could not
do it, anyway.

And there is fire on earth, as promised, whoever
brought it there. People scrape for weeks

to go to Sziget or Burning Man. There is
community, and a theme, and an experience.
And no one gets burnt actually. This fire is
quick to adapt, serviceable, not at all put out
by being put out, reappearing with another coat.
Fire is eternal. And why should not the phoenix
reinvent itself every five years? The market
     changes fast.

It was on the canals this weekend – the energy,
the hope, the longing. But I had no time to
mention it, being inside. Somehow there is a
mismatch, and somehow I am it. But here within
everything went as might be supposed, as if
     there were
no hope and no fury. Except there was a jubilee
which I could not stay for, and a woman fainted
at the prayers of the faithful – too much heat –
     but
she was efficiently transported, and we
     proceeded
as if nothing had transpired, without breaking a
     sweat.

I am only here because I feel
strange, because I could not, for a moment, think
how to distract myself. And if there is an answer
I doubt it can be spoken, and every signpost
can be misleading. I myself am a signpost,

somehow standing inverted at a crossroads
or perhaps a roundabout. I thought … but
nothing is thought through anew, and who
    knows
what the Great Bear thinks.

The fence

the vessels have remained
but the sense has been removed

high heels in the sanctuary
skirt towards the tabernacle
take out the golden crockery
without discerning
the time of the month

"you are to distinguish"
said the raiser of priests
"between the holy and the common"
said the teacher of priests
"between the unclean and the clean"
said the slayer of priests

kosher and treyf
halal and haram
sacred and soiled

the pure and jealous spear of Phinehas
glistening wet at the point
cannot undo the shifts
of seven centuries

the migration
of valuations
of approval
and punishment
of reverence
and anger

what now is the foundation
of the ancient fence
that stands and does not fall?

around the pen of the scapegoats
pitied and admired
with puzzling faith and curious confidence

trying to find a love supreme
a love supreme

all the while
being secret agents
of a promised kingdom

being in the world
without alliance
without partiality
friends without benefits

a safe zone
where all hunts are called off –

gentle sunlight on a still lake

inspired with a message
inflamed with a grace
consumed by a model

harbouring in themselves
the dual polarity
of father sky and mother earth

of the rain and the ground
scattering the seed of words
on all sorts of earths

trying to found a love supreme
a love supreme

Earnest company

I do not treat him right
in his service
his seriousness makes me tense
and breezy and light-hearted
and afraid

the many hours of my education
are like moths around the flame
of his time-honored knowledge
my many doubts like waves
crashing on the rock of his conviction
but not playfully

he is hard of hearing
and difficult of speech
his uncertain smile like sunlight
that hides in guarding clouds
like the clouds
that carry the throne of God

call it holiness or stubbornness
that shows me up
as flighty
as haughty
as disrespectful

as insufficient

to my current
he is inconducive
and inexorably I hear
the crackling of guilt

Singing in the between

my friends make me sing
in soul and body, larynx and diaphragm

travelling to them from Hadrian's Forum
I cross the Limes Aqueduct –
limes, the old imperial border
connecting this northern Rhine
with distant Euphrates
(from the beginning said
to be a river in paradise)
and swirling through the desert
(full of beasts and serpents,
as it says on the map) –

I drive in the middle of the road
I drift in a liminal space
all's measured and numbered and weighted
and my heart shines in my face
for that one rose at the centre
of the limitless empire of ends

travelling from Hadrian's Forum
to sing with my friends

Around the broken law

what violence is covered
by the sleeved robes
of white linen
the *middo vad*

while the high priest
in duplicity and
indecision
gathers the gold
coalesces the calf

his tribe
on second thought
rallies around the broken law
with the hiss of the sword

buying the blessing
at a terrible price

for all purity something is
slain
cut off

denied

how shall a kingdom of priests
trade

how shall a kingdom of priests
marry

how does the Kingdom
relate

Priest at Shiloh

his wrinkled eyes
are without vision

no vision survives
the old experience of age

the seed of waywardness
and wildness continues
its growth – and anger
erodes –

for who would harm a growing thing?

no vision survives
the mild understanding

in its ambiguous sorrow
over the flouted laws
over the harshness of men
over the harshness of god

all the impatience
it cannot for ever outlive

and it accepts the judgment:

tender resignation

from the sanctuary of his wisdom
what came to be?

only
after his death
the naming of his grandchild

Nostalgia

Boy at Shiloh

is he sighing inwardly
in his repetitive action?

hearing a call
hearing: i did not call you

trotting to and fro
in his nightclothes

while the brittle lamp throws
faint shadows on the walls

the old man
sees too little

the young boy
hears too much

like a stock character
in a comedy

hearing and rising
mishearing and returning

ready to respond

when called to service

the time for comedy is over
at Shiloh

the boy is shy to speak the name
of the gathering stormcloud

but he opens the door
and it bursts upon him

The first storms

the first storms of the first summer
static clouds blanketing the brain
a pulse one-and-a-half foot too high
the restlessness of the wandering heart
hovering over the abyss
a bated breath
the suddenness of death
bathed in a livid light of life

in the rumbling, a voice
with abandon
singing of
not abandoning
ever
laughing
remembering
together
sometime
ever

muscles ache
under the stress
of a double protection
of the past
of the present

new things and old
old loyalties and new
and the twofold nature of the new
the twofold possibility of release
they ache

in the ache, a voice
with abandon
singing of
not abandoning
ever
laughing
remembering
together
sometime
ever

Song in a dark place

exploded
a dustcloud
a mesh of particles
each unsure of its own gravity

no core
no artery
a weeping cloud of dryness
barely held together

seared by fire
waterless and déserted
suspended in air

the simple pleasures
are of earth

not at all the place
of current presence

but there are voices
to listen to
to smile at

because a song with two feet on the ground

with deep and sturdy voices
affirms the very rock
of hearty life

no opera
no drama
men as careless as a child
and as confident

At Bethesda

an angel
touched
the water

in the whirlpool
the turbulence
the frantic collision of piled-up waves
was healing

and clarity and frankness and
immersion

it was paradise
it was home
there was I

thrown out
and my legs shattered under me

at Bethesda
having for company
the water still
throbbing
lapping
sloshing

now the waiting
for the water stilling
still
and the passing of You
stopping

then will You ask the question

"do you wish to be well"

and perhaps I shall know
how to reply
beside the still water

A mute spirit speaks

once words appeared

harbingers

I remember when
a sonnet was a banquet

and a meaningful allusion
a hot spark in dry twigs

and the whirling of words in the Word
a vortex to the apex

when words rose higher
than words could express

the last mountain fortress
of elemental joy

and now I stare at sentences
as an old man at fireworks

the cheap sound and fury
on which souls expend themselves

Etude, or askesis

Words clot in the smooth throat;
the old dispensation is passing away.
Is this aridity a perpetual desert,
with meaning gone into exile
to the realm of mute charitable flesh,
where only the brooks' babbling hubbub
recalls the strong-voiced stones of the world's
    hub?
Or is it a purgative way to a clarity
that packs a greater wallop,
reaching from the limit to the goal
fortuitously?

Shall these
Bones live?

Too early I donned
the circlet of the singing tongue.

A good year is left to me
to acquire the Eliotean sense –

or walk with phantom regret in dry lakebeds.

Vox in deserto

Reshaping occurs. The demand of the word
Requires our compresence, as speaking, as
    heard:
It is in the word that we grow more aware –
Poetry is like prayer.

We copy and mimic, translate and distort,
We grow still unknowing how much we fall
    short
(The habit is young; let the critic beware) –
Poetry is like prayer.

And we, when we think we have mastered it,
    falter;
For as our proportions and attitudes alter,
The forms we had fixed fall into disrepair –
Poetry is like prayer.

We thought that our muse had a face; we're not
    sure:
The essence we love is impeccably pure
And we had imagined it pleasantly fair –
Poetry is like prayer.

The words of the world make us hollow at heart;

The words of our past are no fit place to start;
The word that we look for is up in the air –
Poetry is like prayer.

We fidget and itch when we see the white page;
Our quest for sincerity turns into rage
When words do not answer our impotent stare –
Poetry is like prayer.

We dwell in the desert, and each passing day
We question the point and the line of the way.
We look for a shortcut! No shortcut is there –
Poetry is like prayer.

At times we surrender to lateral drift,
Allowing our scope and our focus to shift;
Too far and too fast: and our page is still bare –
Poetry is like prayer.

The poet's fixed patience gives space to the
    word.
Today it may stay still unspoken, unheard;
A noble endeavour refuses despair –
Poetry is like prayer.

Sea of Reeds

Where a thousand vines were – briars. Thorns.
With bow and arrows a man comes there.
    Cautious.
Hawks and porcupines. Hyenas. A screech owl?
These were the names of people who were
    named.
They are dead.
Echoes of wooing and wrath. Cry to Jerusalem
    that
her warfare is ended. For I will gather all the
    nations
against Jerusalem to battle, and the city shall be
    taken
and the houses plundered and the women raped.
    Then
the LORD will come. Jerusalem will dwell in
    security.
O happy day.
I have put my Spirit upon my servant and a
    bruised reed
he will not break. Because you have been a staff
    of reed,
I will bring a sword upon you. I am against you
and will make your land an utter waste and
    desolation

or alternatively I will let you carry on and then
    the end
result will be the same anyway, though it might
    take a little
longer than I am prepared to wait. Immanent
    justice. Karma
is a bitch, says the LORD.
Have we not all one Father? But you have
    married the daughter
of a foreign god. Your eyes have seen what the
    LORD did
at Baal-peor. Take all the chiefs of the people
    and hang them
in the sun before the LORD. Why were you not
    afraid to speak
against my servant Moses? O God, please heal
    her – please.
But the LORD said, If her father had but spit in
    her face,
should she not be shamed seven days? I will
    allure her,
and bring her into the wilderness, and speak
    tenderly to her.
No one shall rescue her out of my hand.
Why do you cry? You are a splintering staff of
    reed,
you and your faithless generation, your sinful
    nation,

all of you are stuck full of splinters and from up
     here
I can hardly see which of them hurt others and
     which
hurt you.
I will tighten your bandages, says the LORD.

Night vision

It is, at the end of the world, disappointing
to be reduced, in the gathering dark, to
seeing the world so indistinctly, blotted, as if
in thermal imaging. One is painfully aware
of limited capacity; a loose stone is not easy
to spot, but significant, lethal perhaps. So
there are things beyond the flashing shapes
that our heated bias alights on. Treading much
more carefully than we would have thought
possible, it is far from clear which signatures
of energy are potentially hostile, or gladdening,
   or
thought-provoking. Shapes have become shades
of wild and gradual hues. Like zones of flames.
Against the wall one cannot quite discern
what huddles there. No face, or shielded by
those yellow arms; looks like the son of a man
perhaps in equal despair, or just very weary,
a thirsty stranger seen in unbearable fire.

I thought the end of the world would be
outlined in white and black. All clearly shaped.

Standing still

and then i stood still

i don't know why
perhaps the water under the bridge
called to the fish in me

i saw
what i had not seen

the currents flowing at their own tranquil speeds
around placid waters
unequal but undivided

a white bird diving under me
and returning again

i felt
what i had not felt
the trembling of the bridge
under my feet

the tree on the river bank
drooped patiently

ducks with combs chattered

skimming across the water
below the bridge

men without combs chatted
overlooking the water
on the other side

the east gate lightly carried
the weight of centuries
through another bright day

i don't know why
and i still stood
still

Aries

Lower your head and mirror that low wall,
unmoved, hard-horned. Now leap! Ahead!
    Surmount
waylaying hedges, rotten trees that fall –
whatever is not vital must not count.
Soak sunlight in your fleece, not for its gold
(which after all you carelessly discard)
but for its startling heat. The spells of cold
in early Spring leave your skin's warmth
    unscarred.
Sacred impatient, rush the meadowlands
in the unquiet vigour of your veins –
see where untouched a fertile foothill stands
that grants a flashing vision of the plains,
and turn to scale the height of your desire
and stamp the hard stone with your hooves of
    fire.